FUQUAN PRESENTS: 30 FOR 30

FUQUAN

Dedicated to Dorothy Gray

Contents

PREFACE

I'm going 30 for 30

 Like this some kind of sport

My words can be the ball

And my page can be the court

Got me bouncing words around

 I'm just trying to make the goal

And even if I can't win the game

Maybe I can touch your soul

The thoughts are in my head

I'm just trying to let them out

Relate to some people

And let them know what I'm about

The game is on the line

With only seconds on the clock

You can say I'm just a writer

That's been known to dodge the block

Crossroads

It's ok to grow

and leave some behind

if you busy you won't notice

and if they love you they won't mind

you can't want it for them

more than they want it for them self

I can't change how you move

it was hard enough changing myself

You see the potential

They see your frustration

They see there's a tomorrow

You just see procrastination

We all have different stories

Which shapes our thoughts

We are the essence of our dreams

And the prisoners of our faults

We can reminisce about the goods times

The jokes and laughs

And embrace our own journey

Hoping again we cross paths

Ambition

Noun

1.   **That thing that separates those that are good from those that are great**

...they gon love you for it

Free Spirit

My spirit is free

But my time is not

So in these 15 minutes

I'm giving it all I got

And it's not for the fame

No I promise it's not

It's about working with a little

And making it a lot

It's about taking some chances

And not second guessing

It's about the days that were dark

And the nights I was stressing

It's about taking something good

And making it better

And if she wants to help me grow

Then I promise I'll let her

The further I get away from distractions

The closer I get to my goals

At first I was getting people to feel me

But now I'm into touching souls

They say it's better to give than receive

So I'm giving it all I got

Because my spirit is free

But my time is not

Got To Keep Reaching

No matter my setbacks

I'm going to keep reaching

If you're listening or not

I'm going to keep preaching

There's too many that's ignorant

So I got to keep teaching

Wondering what hurt Rodney King more

The acquittal or the beating

Society will fool you

And never give you closure

If you want to learn life

It's all about exposure

Try more traveling

And a little more reading

The people you follow

Depicts the life you end up leading

Use your ambition

And find motivation

And focus on the product

But remember presentation

It's Been A Minute

Nowadays when I say good-bye

It might come with some tears

I told some people see you later

And I ain't seen them in years

It didn't happen on purpose

That was not the intention

We didn't take the same route

So we aren't in the same position

I know I got to keep pushing

Any doubt will leave you stranded

Success is not given

It only happens when you plan it

Stop thinking about jobs

And think more about careers

I told some people see you later

And I haven't seen them in years

Energy

Noun

1.   **That thing I don't waste on unimportant matters**

...they trying to drain me of it

Martin & Maya

I'm dreaming like Martin, I'm rising like Maya

If I told you I'm a hustler, I'd be preaching to the choir

Heart kind of cold, but my soul on fire

Working hard now, so I can relax when I retire

Gaining more knowledge, while increasing my desire

Working with the scraps, trying to build an empire

Growth and profitability, are the things that I admire

Focusing on the future, letting go of what was prior

You need some motivation, I'll be your supplier

I'm dreaming like Martin, and I'm rising like Maya

Maybe

You lied and cheated and caused her stress

And thought that things would stay the same

You both fell in love for the wrong reasons

So right now is hard to say who's to blame

Maybe if she understood you more

Or maybe if love didn't make you fall

Or maybe the truth of the matter is

Maybe you never really loved her at all

Or maybe you did but in your own way

And it was clearly a way she didn't understand

And maybe to fully love her the way she wanted

You had to leave boyhood and become a man

There's nothing more fulfilling

Than a man truly loving his lady

It can make the world a better place

If we can make it there, Maybe

Don't involve the kids

He said don't take them away from me

Don't use the kids against me

If you want to cover me with bad father skills

Then maybe God will be the one to rinse me

Just because we didn't work out

Doesn't mean we can't be adults about it

Raise our kids to be best of our ability

And make sure not to have our judgment clouded

He said I'm just trying to see my kids

But all you're thinking is child support

It's obvious it's a money thing

And you have no idea of the battles I've fought

Now I'm in court

Trying to up my visiting rights

While you're on social media

Trying to up your Instagram likes

As far as our broken relationship

It is what it is

Just do me a favor

And don't involve the kids

Proph(i)ts

I met a brotha that said he used to go to church

But then he had to stop it

Cause it seemed like the prophet preaching the sermon

Main concern was making a profit

I had to think about it for a minute

And realize where he was coming from

He said he seen more collection plates than blessings

And every church just seemed like the other one

He said I paid my tithes

I joined the choir

I was even on the deacon board

But the more of my money I gave to the church

The further away I felt from the Lord

He said don't get me wrong

I love the Lord and I still believe in Jesus Christ

But to go and visit him in his house

I shouldn't have to pay a price

Things have changed nothings the same

Now it just seems like a circus act

The church on TV, the pastor got a book deal

And every year he buys a new Cadillac

He said take me back to big mama church

Where the choir had the whole place stomping their feet

Sister Johnson caught the Holy Ghost 2 or 3 times

And after church you could probably get a plate to eat

He said I'm not trying to discourage you brotha

If want to go don't let me stop it

I'd just rather be somewhere

That makes a bigger difference than a bigger profit

Rat Race

All I'm just trying to do

Is get out the rat race

Some say life is sweet

I'm trying to see how that taste

Don't know the Jones' personally

But I'm trying to keep up with that pace

Making sure make hair is cut

Just so I can show face

The lights are on

But I'm still in a dark place

Creating my own path

Because I vowed that I would not trace

The blunt already rolled

How can I trust that it's not laced

They said I used to be a hot head

But right now that's a cold case

Trying to be Paid in Full

I think I'm part Mitch and part Ace

All I'm trying to do, is get out of the rat race

Same Ol' G

I'm the same person

My hustle just changed

So the next time you see me

Please don't look at me strange

Don't judge me from my past

I've updated that person

I've been soaking up the knowledge

And steadily reimbursing

I've traveled a bit

I've gained some exposure

I've dealt with my demons

And given them closure

I have a new target

I've extended my range

I'm the same Ol' G

My perspective just changed

She was dope to me

She was dope to me,

And she already knew that

Trials and tribulations

We had already been through that

I guess I hung around Saints

She was always saying "who dat"?

Love and happiness

I figured we might as well pursue that

She didn't go with the crowd

And I always knew where she was coming from

I could chill with her all day

And not just think about getting some

We knew what each other was thinking

But we didn't become predictable

And all the love that was given

We made sure it was reciprocal

We looked out for each other

Like two cops during a stake out

She knew her way around the kitchen

But didn't believe in having her cakes out

She was a Nubian queen

So she always represented that

She had high self-esteem

And vowed not to let anyone limit that

I valued her opinion and listened close

When she spoke to me

I got high off her every day

no drugs involved

She was dope to me

Effort

Noun

1.That thing that shows your level of interest

...that's all I'm asking for

Started From The Bottom

You can't talk down to me

Because I know what the bottom feels like

And because of stuff I've felt in the past

I know when shit don't feel right

My Spidey senses are tingling

But that's a natural reflex

Don't get caught up in the cover

It's more about the context

Growing wiser day to day

That is just a goal of mine

Knowing when it's time to fold

And knowing when to cross the line

Chest to the sky

With my fist clinched tight

You can't talk down to me

Because I know what the bottom feels like

Sweat Shop

Once I get inside you,

I promise that I'll go slow

I'll satisfy you so much

You'll want to let the world know

Licking, pulling, choking, smacking,

And that's just part of foreplay

Have you walking funny

While you're looking for the doorway

I'll adjust your attitude

Have you in kitchen more

Half the time you're cooking

The other half we on the kitchen floor

Your buns on the counter

With my sausage in your soft spot

Juices everywhere

We turned the kitchen to a sweat shop

Passion

Noun

1. **That reason nobody had to ask or tell you to do it**

...turn your passion into a profit

Take Me As I Am

Take me as I am,

Or leave me where you found me

At this point in my life

I just need the positive around me

I can't say that enough

Cause I feed off the energy

And you don't have to like science

To understand chemistry

I'm careful who I talk to

And with whom I stay surrounded

My friends help hype me up

My family helps keep me grounded

With no hesitation

I say this profoundly

Take me as I am

Or you can leave me where you found me

There was a Struggle Involved

The person you see today is okay

But before this, there was a struggle involved

A couple dark holes I had to climb out of

A couple puzzles I had to solve

A couple habits I had to kick

A couple of corners I had to bend

A couple ties I had to sever

A couple of battles I had to win

There were some nights I couldn't sleep

There were some folks I couldn't trust

There were some deadlines I didn't meet

A couple of bubbles of mine that bust

But I grew through the process

So I can say that I evolved

The person you see today is okay

But there was a struggle involved

To Know Me

To know me

Is to love me

And to love me

Is a challenge

I'm on my Libra scale

Still trying to find balance

Taking what I'm given

While steadily pursuing

I was underestimated

So I'm into overdoing

I'm into overthinking

But my answers can be trusted

I'm into solving problems

So if it's an issue we'll discuss it

Sarcasm is my go-to

So it's pretty hard to read me

I don't work well with others

But I'm here if you need me

Prayer

Noun

1.That thing you use to talk to God

...highly recommended for daily usage

She Following Me

No social media,

she said she following me

she was less impressed with the fame

but more so the college degree

I was impressed with her conversation

It always started with "we"

which means she seen me in her future

which wasn't a problem for me

all I asked is that she keep it solid with me

no comparisons to her past and how she thought it would be

they say love don't cost a thing

so what I'm giving is free

I want to make you my queen

the way you keep honoring me

what she gives me is real

I don't live off perceptions

she said she is following me

so she doesn't need any directions

Top of the Key

I'm not afraid to go after it

Even if it's a long shot

Cause even if I don't make it

Regrets is something I don't got

Just because it didn't work for others

Does not affect my outcome

Basing my life off of someone else's

To me that shit just sounds dumb

I know life has no guarantees

And that's the reason I stay prepared

The way I look adversity in the face

You would swear that I was never scared

You can call me a dream chaser

That's trying to create his own spot

Cause see I'm not afraid to go after it

Even if it's a long shot

Tough Love

Why can't I be successful

Without there being a circumstance

Cause now if I get a felony on my record

It's unlikely the world will give me a second chance

So my every move is calculated

I think before I react to stuff

Cause one false move and you'll surely see

That the love the world gives is always tough

Innocent until proven guilty

Is not a law that applies to us

So it's a catch 22 with whatever we do

In trying to decide which lies we trust

Never issued a BDU

But suffered from PTSD

And no one ever took the time of day

To see what was really bothering me

Another statistic lost in the system

Body is present but the heart is missing

It's easy to see that the love was tough

When it's hard to get anyone in the world to listen

Tropical Fruit

My purpose for trying to make it

Is so you can feel me and not see me

Famous enough that you know who I am

But I can still move freely

I'm trying to be remote

I'm talking somewhere without a TV

Yeah somewhere exotic

Where they grow pineapples and kiwi

Somewhere that I can't take my thoughts

And remember not to pack the drama

Just a pen and a pad

And a couple quotes from the Dalai Lama

A place with green grass, blue skies

And a couple of waterfalls

With your soft skin, brown eyes

And some happily ever after alls

Pride

Noun

1.That thing that will have you missing out on shit

...don't let pride cost you the prize

Teamwork Makes The Dream Work

She said why you expect me to cook and clean,

and still hold down a 9 to 5

he said shorty I don't really have expectations

I was just trying to keep hope alive

he said being domestic is part of life

and going to work makes you independent

you being an example to the future generation

is really was all that was ever intended

I'm just trying to bring out the best in you

And don't come off as critical

But I guess my suggestions seem like directions

And you take them as atypical

We in this race together my lady

My goal is for us to be leading the pack

And if one of us ever hits a bump

The other is there to keep up on track

The Huxtables

I trusted you so I discussed with you

us living life like a Huxtable

a couple of kids

and maybe a truck or two

and if you don't like living up north

then the south will do

we can have a house in Atlanta

and some property in Cali

and when we take vacations

it's to places like Maui

mindset the same

we focused on growing

and the moves that we make

aren't for anybody knowing

We can have a little Rudy

And Maybe a Theo

I am a Libra

So you're probably a Leo

Our minds are both open

Just like the lines of communication

And our legacy will last

Cause we'll have a solid foundation

You Can Do It

I know I can do it

I just have to take the first step

Results will soon follow

You just got to do the first rep

Obstacles will show face

But that's what they made endurance for

Look at life like tuna fish

It's that regular shit then there's albacore

The more that you put into it

The easier it is to reach your goal

Things may seem to get out of hand

But the victorious one is the one in control

Keep your mind clear

That's where all the best ideas are kept

No matter how long the journey is

The process trumps the final step

I Overdosed

Lately I been getting high off me

And no not in a selfish way

But I looked at the time I've put into us

And figured I had some dues to pay

I noticed a lot of things we did

Didn't bring out the best in me

And one thing I vowed I would never do

Is settle for complacency

No I'm not saying anything is wrong with you

This is truly a reflection of myself

And sometimes we get put in someone's life

To make us better for someone else

Telling you its over

Was one of the hardest things I ever had to do

And the best apology

Is you never ever having to

The things we take for granted

Are the things we seem to miss the most

I'm sorry it had to end this way

But I been getting high off me and I overdosed

Unhappy Vows

Its crazy cause nights she laid next to me

Is when I really felt lonely

And when she told people she was happy

That shit sounded phony

And instead of a love interest

She felt more like a homie

Like the vows we made were processed

In other words a bunch of bologna

The pettiness has got to stop

It's like what the hell are we fighting for

And I never had dreams of being an author

But lately I've found myself writing more

I can't really say when shit went south

Or if I was the cause of it

But it feels like we're watching our relationship destruct

And ain't nobody pausing it

If I could do things all over again

I probably would run my same course

See just because you place your bet

Doesn't mean you'll choose the winning horse

Relationships are hard enough

But they're even harder when they're missing smiles

When mama said it would be days like this

I had no idea about unhappy vows

Live with purpose

He said this thing called life

is not what I expected

but before my last breath

I plan to have this thing perfected

everything happens for a reason

so he couldn't help but respect it

and even though Kanye might've been joking

he'd feel safer if he was elected

he viewed the world different

from the age 22 to 32

and you would have to know where he came from

to know exactly what he was going through

he was a risk taker

so he traveled the unbeaten path

he wouldn't mind peace

but a piece of mind is something he'd rather have

he was a product of his environment

and his environment was the inner city

he said you can learn about me by riding the wave

but to get to know me you'd have to be walking with me

the road was long and the streets were tough

but that's what makes the journey worth it

he wasn't necessarily trying to make history

but rather build his legacy and then try to preserve it

he just wanted to get the most out of life

and also provide the world a service

and when everything was over and done

his headstone would read "he lived with purpose"

Purpose

Noun

1.The thing that once you find it makes life complete

...I had my reasons, now I just needed a purpose

The Test of Life

He said I get more out of life

when you think less of me

like you finding out I'm a lawyer

after arresting me

it's like putting me in a bad position

is when you get the best of me

and I don't need a scantron

to know if you are testing me

It's like even when I'm right

The world be second guessing me

It's like one day they were praising me

And the next day they were stressing me

But as long as I keep believing

The Lord will keep on blessing me

Taking all of my shortcomings

And turning them into ecstasy

some may take this as a testimony

but for others it's a recipe

it depends if you believe life is predestined

or if you believe you create your own destiny

Deeper Than Sex

He said I want to get to know you

but I keep running into roadblocks

you blow things out of proportion

like you addicted to using Botox

I'm not the thirsty type

so "you look nice" is just a compliment

but because of how dudes treated you in past

with my words I got to be cognizant

I know the world has made you independent

So having a man is just a plus

But captions that read "single and living"

Will never sound as good as "This is Us"

I want to know what you're all about

with no relation to wanting sex

but life has showed you to guard your heart

with blocks of ice and safety nets

I want to discuss your 5-year plan

and how to make our community strong

cause truth be told if the conversation off

then you can keep your panties on

He Went Deep Like Poetry

She said the way you feel inside of me

is nothing short of poetry

the way you put your stamp on it

you should've been a notary

hands tied legs spread

I'll let you take control of me

she said I want you deep inside

fucking up my ovary

don't hold nothing back

fill me with your inhibition

a race to see who bust first

treat it like a competition

thighs wrapped around your torso

squeezing like a bear hug

started on a Posturepedic

ended on a bear rug

Feeling like a love jones

Living out a fantasy

If crazy fucking is the charge

I got to plead insanity

Good Girl Gone Bad

I tried to play the good guy

she said she already had those

good girl gone bad

she addicted to the assholes

she had a couple flaws

but I was willing to look pass those

helping her see that good fertilizer

is the reason why the grass grows

attention to the details

nurturing the process

those who expect the most

Always end up with a lot less

tragedies are casualties

that could have had a better plan

and bitter women are daddy's girls

that wish they had a better man

The energy she gives off

Is a reflection of her state of mind

So if she knew what her future held

She would have let that bad boy stay behind

Website:
Fuquanthepoet.com

Instagram:
@Fuquanthepoet_

Twitter:
@Fuquanthepoet_

www.ingramcontent.com/pod-product-compliance
Lightning Source LLC
LaVergne TN
LVHW051430080426
835508LV00022B/3336